THE RETURN OF SHETTIMA

THE BOY SLAVE

KOLA ONADIPE

Contents

Introduction

If you have not met Shettima dan Gatta, let him now be introduced. Shettima grew up in a happy family in the village of Birnin Boko in Northern Nigeria. His father, the Fulani, Gattama Boko, was frail, weak and handsome. His mother was stout and strong. She ruled the home. His sister Halima, the most senior of his three sisters, loved him very much. He loved her in return.

At eight, while inspecting his snares or traps in the bush, Shettima was kidnapped. He was taken first to Garin Bassam where Shehu Minchika, the great slave dealer, lived above the law. Shettima was sold into slavery with other children and taken to Tulin Goma, a travellers' village on the edge of the desert. Here he met Al Atiku the only son and heir of Sheik

Maitama who lived in Yelua and was next in rank to the Sultan. The Sheik was rich and powerful. He bought slaves to provide labour on his plantations, on his grazing fields and in the travellers' village.

Back in Birnin Boko, after a fruitless search for Shettima, Gattama Boko had wept for the loss of his only son. He wept too because there would be no son to wield the famous sword of his own father, a famous warrior, no one to win fame and glory for the family, He did not survive the loss of Shettima. He died while looking for his son. He waited for heaven and to bring him back home. He was sure that Shettima would come back one day and wield the famous sword.

Both Shettima's mother and his sister Halima believed Gattama and looked forward to Shettima's return, Meanwhile, Shettima lived in slavery after only a day on the plantation; he saved Al Atiku from an attack by Matamba, the ruthless head slave. He was rewarded for this by the Sheik who transferred him to work with the travellers: Here he learnt to ride and to speak different languages. He met people of different races and saw both the bright and dark sides of human nature and life,

After several years Shettima met two travellers from Shahin, the home village of his mother. They carried home the news of Skettima's wellbeing and brought back love from his mother and sisters and a parcel of baked milk cake from Halima. However, they failed to persuade Shettima to escape because he was well treated and felt that he had nothing to escape from.

Eventually, however, Shettima had to escape? From the anger of his friend, Al Atiku, because of a love tangle with Sherifat, the Sheik's daughter, and Fatima, her maid!

Because Shettima fell in love with Fatima and did not return Sherifat's love, the Sheik's daughter fell ill.

Her brother, Al Atiku, was very angry with Shetima for harming his sister and challenged him to a duel. Because he wanted to avoid the deadly duel, Shettima escaped in the night. His horse ran into a pit across his path and was trapped. Shettima had no heart to desert his horse, and he knew he would not get far on foot. His escape was blocked.

Al Atiku, accompanied by two of his servants, pursued Shettima; they too fell into the ditch with Shettima. Rather than run away or avenge himself on the injured party, Shettima helped to nurse their wounds and to rescue the trapped horses. This convinced Al Atiku of Shettima's innocence. When the Sheik sat in judgment over Shettima on the charges of running away and offences against the Sheik's son and daughter, Al Atiku stood in his defence and softened the heart of the Sheik.

"Both my son and daughter have pleaded for you," said the Sheik, "and I have never refused the requests of my children. You will not be as planned. Because you have saved my son's life twice, I will not take your life. In gratitude I give you your freedom."

1. Shettima and Fatima are freed

It was difficult for me to trust my ears. I could not believe that not only was I not going to be punished for the charges made against me but that I was free. The change was so sudden that I thought that I must be dreaming. I hardly heard his last sentence in my astonishment but I smiled. I stood there and looked around. There were people standing and murmuring and, I suspect, looking forward to watching my punishment. I did not know how to take their silence. They too must have been surprised at the sudden change in my fortune.

Those who sat around the Sheik and made up his court also shared in this mood. There was a strange silence in the courtyard. Suddenly the Sheik rose. This jerked those around him as it were, back to life. Soon everybody was talking

Their murmuring brought me back to reality; and in my mind there was just one thought.

Fatima! I looked up and the Sheik was watching me. I realised he was waiting for a reply to that half-heard question:

"Is there any other thing you would wish to ask for?"

"If I may be as bold as to ask, will you please set Fatima free also?"

"Yes! She too is free," answered the Sheik.

After that I did not care what happened. The whole world might be in bondage as long as Fatima and I were free. I am sorry to admit this, but perhaps I would have chosen Fatima rather than my whole family in Birnin Boko.

The Sheik walked away surrounded by his courtiers. The disappointed spectators wandered away too. No one came near me to share with me the joy of my escape and the gift of my freedom. Soon the yard was once again empty. I stood there alone. I did not know what to do. I had my freedom but what was I to do with it? It is the strange irony of this life that the value of a thing is greater to us before we have it than its value once we have obtained it. Except that the freedom would enable me to have Fatima as a wife it seemed to have no other value.

If I remained in Tulin Goma or even in Yelua, what else could I do other than work for the Sheik. I would work with the same people with whom I had worked as a slave. I would visit the same places. Life would be just the same. I could hardly be happier than I had been as a favoured slave. If I went back home to Birnin Boko, I would have to start all over again. Life there would hardly be exciting. I was now a man and all those things that made my childhood there happy and exciting could not touch me anymore. I could not imagine what type of life 1 could provide for Fatima.

These thoughts raced through my mind as I stood there as if bound by a spell. My eyes were open but I did not seem to see anything around me. Nor did my ears hear anything. I was buried in my own thoughts. I started when I felt a hand on my shoulder.

"Shettima! Wake up!" said a voice.

I turned around and there was Al Atiku, his face lit by a smile. Here once again was the same Al Atiku that I used to know before his sister came between us. The picture of our meeting when he challenged me to a duel and spat on my face came up in my mind and stood side by side with the present. It was difficult to believe that only three days had passed between one and the other. Indeed, man is both a beast and an angel and what goes on in his mind decides which role he plays at a particular time.

I looked Al Atiku in the face but I could not speak. My mouth tried to shape the words but there was no sound. "Let me congratulate you," Al Atiku continued, seeing my confusion. "The truth will always come out, no matter how late. I am sorry for the part I played, but you will understand: Blood is thicker than water. You probably would have done the same if you had been me. Let us forget the episode, for what is past is past and all's well that ends well. You have already been rewarded with the greatest gift that the Sheik can give and which any man can have: the gift of freedom. Let us now return to our old friendship."

I had not come to hate Al Atiku in spite of all the wrong that I had suffered. Even when I knew that he hated me because of his sister, I had not been able to hate him. He had done much for me since I had come as a slave to his father's establishment. 1 owed all the training, all the comfort and every good thing I had to him and to his friendship. If he had killed me I would, while dying, still not have hated him.

He stretched forth his two hands as a gesture of friendship and I went to him fondly. Two large tears rolled down my face, tears of joy: Joy at this coming together again. We did not remain there long. He turned and I followed. We were sitting in his apartment before I realised that I had never before stepped into this place. As a slave I could not go there unless I was invited to serve. This then was the first proof of my new status. But strangely enough, as soon as I realised this, I became uncomfortable. What did I have to give in return as one free man to another? It was then that it dawned on me that I had nothing in this world, not even the tools for making the simplest article. I had not, of my own, even the food to eat or the clothes to wear. If Fatima was set free in her rags, how was I to clothe her?

If I was to go on enjoying the same standard of living I was now used to, I would have to depend on the kindness of Al Atiku and the Sheik. If this kindness did not continue, I would have to work for a wage. This would not be much and certainly would not be enough to keep me in the way to which I had become accustomed as a favoured slave.

I now knew that freedom might be a good thing but some forms of freedom could be worse than slavery. We sat down there in his apartment. He was very free and open, but I was as uneasy as if I had been sitting on thorns. It was not easy for me to get used to this sudden rise in my status. It was with difficulty that he persuaded me to sit with him on his mat and eat with him from the same dish. I did not like it when his slaves held the bowl of water and waited for me to wash my hands before and after the meal. Having been a slave myself, and knowing the feelings of a slave, I could never accept a slave's services with pleasure.

After the meal we sat down on leather cushions and talked. Al Atiku was making every effort to help me forget my recent experience and make me accept my new status easily. As if he could read my mind he asked me:

"What now is your plan for the future? Do you remain here or do you go back home?"

"That is my headache right now. It is not going to be easy to decide. Going home means exchanging certainty for uncertainty; it may mean exchanging a life of ease for a life of toil and hardship. It will mean leaving old friends and known ways. Who knows what the new ones will be like? But to remain here would not be real freedom. I would be working in the same surroundings in which I have served as a slave and would feel as if I belonged to the same old master. It would hardly be freedom. I would have enslaved myself instead of being enslaved."

"I can see how your mind is working and I cannot blame you. But you will have to decide quickly so that we can plan the business here," he said.

"I wonder how soon Fatima will be freed. It will be difficult for me to make decisions alone from now on. I need her to help me decide," I answered.

"Fatima will soon be freed," he answered.

Meanwhile, unknown to us steps were already being taken to set Fatima free. But Fatima knew nothing of what had happened. She knew nothing about my flight. She knew nothing about my trial and sufferings. She knew nothing about our freedom. Living now in the lowest rank among slaves, she had spoken very little to anyone except when it was necessary. She had accepted her punishment bravely and she did not invite pity or accept sympathy from anyone.

Fatima was working in the kitchen when Sherifat's maid, Salamat, came to tell her the news, excited and smiling. Fatima turned from her and continued her work.

"I have good news for you, Fatima," said Salamat, her voice shaking with excitement. The other slaves around straightened up to listen as if it was they who were addressed. "You are to change into a better dress and come with me to the mistress."

Fatima wanted to refuse to go, but she knew she could not. But she did refuse to change her dress:

"I was sent here by our mistress in these rags and she must see me in them," she said. "Please yourself," answered Salamat a bit angrily. "Come with me."

When they appeared before Sherifat in the bright light of her apartment, Fatima's rags looked even drabber. The slaves who waited on Sherifat withdrew quietly one after the other, their hands over their mouths to hide their smiles. Their giggles reached Fatima ears as they left the room. But this did not worry Fatima. She had told herself many times that she was a slave and a slave had no honour and so could feel no disgrace or shame. Slavery itself was the very opposite of honour.

She felt sorry for these slaves who felt that because they were more cleanly dressed, they were any better.

"Salamat, did I not ask that Fatima be brought before me in a clean dress?" asked Sherifat.

"She would not change from this," Salamat answered.

"And why?" asked Sherifat.

"Is my mistress not pleased to see me in these rags? It was you who commanded that I should be thus dressed," answered Fatima. "Why must I be different here from where you have sent me? These rags suit my station in life better than borrowed dresses." At that moment one of the slaves returned. Fatima pointed at her:

"Look at her clothes. They are a joke on her. A decorated slave is not only a slave but also a big fool. She lives in two worlds, neither of which is real. She is up this moment, and the next she is down. Kindness to a slave can never last long. It is never true. If you buy someone into slavery, why give her kindness in slavery unless it is meant to get harder work out of her?" "I did not bring you here to give me a lesson," said Sherifat. "Perhaps much of what you have said is true, perhaps not. I can understand your bitterness though I will need time to understand your thoughts. You have had plenty of time to think on these things. But now I have news for you."

"What news can there be for a slave?" asked Fatima.

"The truth, Fatima, is that you are no longer a slave," answered Sherifat. "The Sheik has ordered that you be set free."

Fatima stood there and said nothing. There was a strange silence for a while.

It was the thought of me: Shettima, which filled Fatima's mind just then. She thought that her freedom was worthless ifI was not freed.

At last Fatima broke the silence: "Where is Shettima?" she demanded.

"I knew you would ask," answered Sherifa "He too has been freed."

Then, in spite of herself, Fatima ran toward Sherifat and embraced her. She wept. Sherif understood her feelings and tried to comfort by holding her warmly, ignoring her filthy rags.

At last Fatima pulled herself away.

"I am sorry," she said. "I could not stop myself."

The news had softened the heart of Fatima and all her hatred for Sherifat and sorrow melted away. Now when she spoke there was no bitterness.

"Allah be praised," Fatima said. "I never thought I would know this joy again. If Salamat will give me a change of dress now I will gladly take it."

"You must wash first," answered Sherifat. "If you go into my bathroom, you will find everything ready for you. You still know your way; nothing has changed except that now, instead of you waiting on me, someone will wait on you.'

2. Marriage

Back in their room the slave girls spoke not a word. They sat down, folded their arms round their raised knees and rested their bent heads on their knees. Their sorrow was great. They had just seen one of the wonders of this life. They had just seen one of the changes of which this life is full and which no one can predict. They had seen Fatima, who some days earlier was disgraced and degraded, at whose misfortune they had laughed, eating from the same pot with the same mistress who they made to hate her. Yet with her new free status, she would not let them, who had betrayed her, degrade themselves.

After the meal, Sherifat told Fatima the story of the events which led to her freedom. Sherifat told the story without any bitterness.

She now knew the truth about the part which Fatima played and had no cause to blame her. She no longer felt angry towards me, Shettima, because she had herself seen the folly of her heart.

"What is your plan for the future now?" she asked Fatima just as her brother had asked me. But, unlike me, Fatima was ready with her answer. She knew what she wanted and she had no doubt that I would do as she wanted:

"Shettima and I are going to get married here right away and after that we go away to his home," answered Fatima. Sherifat seemed to be turning something over in her mind. Fatima, as if she read her mind, continued:

"Perhaps you are wondering how we are going to make a living now? If that is it, don't worry. We will find a way."

Sherifat smiled at the girl's assurance:
"Well, let me see what Shettima has to say."

"Oh yes! Where is Shettima? I am dying
to see him. I have seen him only twice and I
have hardly spoken to him. Yet I seem to have
known him all my life and the whole of my
future is tied up with him."

"You will not have long to wait. He is
with my brother at this moment and only very
few walls divide you from him whom your
heart seeks. It is the man who seeks the woman
or else I should have asked that we go to him."

Sherifat was right. As if she saw through
the walls, Al Atiku and I were even then on the
way to her apartment and almost immediately
she heard her brother's footsteps:

"Here they come," she said. Fatima
looked round. The door opened and she saw Al
Atiku but she also saw towering above him -

my face which she would have recognized in the dark. She was amazed that she knew every line of my face since she had only met me very briefly on two occasions.

There were four of us, the brother and sister and the two newly freed slaves, but there was silence too. It seemed as if we were stricken dumb. Each looked at the others and waited for someone else to say something. Nobody seemed to know what to say. Both Al Atiku and Sherifat expected us, the two lovers, to do or say something, for they felt that they had played their parts in bringing us together. Fatima waited for me to make a move. She expected me to come forward and embrace her and then she would return the warmth. But I did no such thing. I simply stood there looking intently on her face. The expression on my face showed clearly how happy and at the same time how shy I was. What should I say to her before other people?

But Fatima was brave. She broke the silence. She called out to me, almost shouting: "Come on! Why are you waiting? Have we not waited long enough?"

Almost at once, as if drawn suddenly by a cord, I stepped forward and Fatima and I were locked in a close embrace. Al Atiku and Sherifat withdrew silently from the room so we could speak freely to each other:

"Is it well with you? Are you happy? Have you not suffered much?" I asked one question after another and did not wait for an answer.

"I am well, Shettima," she answered quietly. "All's well that ends well. Who would have thought that I would be free? It is too good to be true. Hold me once more so that I may believe it."

Come on! Why are you waiting?

We were alone for a long while. We spoke about many things, but above all we planned our future. Fatima was in no doubt as to what she wanted. For her there was no question of remaining in the Sheik's establishment. She had lived many years there as a slave and she saw the whole place with the eyes of a slave. It was impossible for her to remain there and not feel and think like a slave. Everything and everybody would remind her of her past. She must live in a different place to be able to feel free and enjoy to the full this freedom.

Because Fatima wanted it and because I had no better plan to put forward, I readily agreed. We had to leave. For where? The only place was home, in Birnin Boko. Fatima did not remember where her home was because she had been kidnapped when she was too young to know. She remembered nothing about herself before she was a slave. She did not even know how she came by the name she bore. My home was therefore her home. She would have the opportunity and the joy of having a home for the first time in her life. She would gladly be a wife in that home, however poor.

But before setting out for home, Fatima and I decided to get married. We did not want a grand marriage of the type we had seen among the free people around. We had nothing but each other and even the food we ate came as a gift from the Sheik's children. How could we feed guests at a wedding? Fortunately there could be marriage without the elaborate ceremony. All that was necessary was the desire of both parties to get married and the prayer of a Malam. There was no one to receive the bride price since Fatima had no parents.

When Al Atiku and Sherifat returned to the room Fatima and I told them our plan. We were to be married the following day and to set off homewards the day after. We looked so happy that there was nothing in our faces to show that we were worried about the difficulties which we would face and the uncertainties of the journey and of life in Birnin Boko. Al Atiku and his sister realised that it would do no good to raise these questions and that I was too proud to ask for any help. But they decided to give us some pleasant surprises.

On the following day Al Atiku led me to the mosque. There a crowd was already gathered and there before him stood Fatima and Sherifat hand in hand. Fatima was very happy. She smiled as her eyes met mine.

I waved to her. I had no doubt about who had made these arrangements and I was filled with gratitude to both Al Atiku and Sherifat.

The ceremony was a short one. The people were entertained and the crowd dispersed. My wife and I did not feel happy about leaving our friends and the places we had known. It was like going away from light into darkness. But in that darkness was Birnin Boko, our home. There I would have every right of a son of the soil.

Before sunrise the following morning, Fatima and I woke up and got ourselves ready to start on our journey. I still had my horse which had by now recovered from the injuries she had sustained when she fell into the pit. She had caught the mood of our excitement and flicked her tail and pawed the ground with her hooves. She neighed as if she was calling on me to hurry.

When I went to wake up Al Atiku who had been our host for that night, I found to my surprise that he was up and dressed. His horse was waiting outside, and with it were his two servants who, with him, had chased me on the day of my escape.

"Where are you going?" I asked. "You are dressed for a journey."

"I am going with you part of the way. It is the least I can do for a friend," Al Atiku answered.

I said nothing, but I knew that Al Atiku knew what was in my mind.

When I returned with Al Atiku and his servants to where I had left my horse, I saw Fatima standing not alone as I had expected, but with Sherifat. She too was dressed for a journey. This time I did not ask any questions because I knew the answer. Without further words the group moved out of the courtyard.

The first part of the journey was over familiar ground for it was from Yelua to Tulin Goma. Beyond Tulin Goma for several miles it was still familiar ground. Here Al Atiku and I raced our horses and played many boyish pranks. As we went sober this time over the ground, we recalled the pleasant times we had

had here and thought with some regret that these times would never return.

After a long ride we came to places which were strange to us. The grass here was green and the trees were closer together than in the near- desert around Tulin Goma. We met a few people who greeted us cheerfully.

It was almost noon when we stopped under the shade of a Shea-butter tree. At the request of Al Atiku the servants undid one of the saddle-bags. They soon set before us a pot of delicious food. We ate happily together.

Now it was time to part. We all stood up and held hands with each other.

"I don't know how far from here your home is, Shettima, but I have a feeling that we shall meet again," said Al Atiku. "My two servants went all the way. Accept these gifts you will go which I make you and which my sister makes Fatima in token of our love. You will need something to start you on a new life when you get home."

"I cannot say how much I am indebted to you," I replied. "I do not know how I shall ever repay you for the kindness you have shown to me. Someday, perhaps, you will need me and then you need only call me. I will answer you readily. But take this one piece of advice from me: Go and find yourself a wife without delay; you need a companion."

"I will do as you have said," he answered. "I envy you and I hope I will find a good woman like Fatima for a wife."

Sherifat and Fatima did not speak much but before parting Fatima embraced Sherifat and thanked her for the gifts.

The parting was painful to the four of us and for a long time we turned back and waved our hands in farewell.

Soon each was lost to the other in the distance but the memories of the past lived with us. The longing for a meeting which was born in us then grew stronger and stronger and when we were out of one another's sight we were not out of one another's minds.

3. Shehu Minchika's Hospitality

This indeed was the real beginning of the journey back home, although the two servants were still a link between us and the Sheik's establishment. But now we were at last truly setting out on our path to freedom.

The servants, who were not strangers to me and who had witnessed the various changes in my fortune, were very understanding and willing. They did everything to make us both comfortable, but they did even more for my wife. If she had been a queen she could not have received greater attention. Seeing Fatima happy and well cared for was a great pleasure to me. It was a relief too because I had been worried about how she would endure such a long journey.

After parting with Al Atiku and his sister our journey was less leisurely. I had a general idea of the direction and a description of certain places on the way. I remembered that the journey had taken three days when I was taken into slavery. I had therefore expected that it would take no less than three days to get back home. But at the rate we were now going I knew that we would reach home soonest.

Late that night we arrived at Minisallah, a small village with an inn where travellers could pass the night. Hardly anything was provided for our comfort.

We were shown into a miserable room. No light was provided and it was very warm. Happily there was a ladder by which we climbed up to the flat roof. The roof was partly mud and partly thatch but it was strong enough to carry our weight. Here we had a light meal and slept. Because there was no mat, Fatima lay on the goat skin on which I used to say my prayers. I spread Fatima's spare wrapper on the hard roof and lay on it.

But we were so tired, we were happy to lie down anywhere. I lay close to Fatima and because we were together, we forgot everything and everybody else. We forgot the hard floor on which we slept. Even while we slept, we held hands; perhaps we wished that even in the dreamland we would move around holding hands.

In the morning we were thoroughly refreshed in mind and body. Fatima looked very beautiful in spite of her rough hair. Soon we set out once again, hoping to reach Birnin Boko that day.

As we set out that morning, I saw a new light in Fatima's face. The joy within her seemed to shine through her eyes. And when she asked me excitedly: "Will we really reach Birnin Boko today?" the light shone more brightly. When I answered her: "By the grace of Allah, we shall make it," she settled down in perfect peace.

What a wonderful girl I had for a wife! Here she was in a strange land, going to a destination about which she knew nothing and instead of being frightened, she was calm and happy. Now I know that once a good woman trusts, she trusts absolutely and she will continue to trust till she finds a strong reason for not trusting or until she ceases to be good.

But it was not just that alone. Fatima was different from other women. I was convinced that when they were sharing our confidence and courage at creation she went with a basket. In place of a handful she had a basketful. This quality was to support me often in the future, for while I was not a coward, she induced that

40

excess of courage which distinguishes heroes from ordinary people. And even now as we went homewards, Fatima's calmness was not only a challenge to me. It was an inspiration.

While I was busy turning over these things in my mind, the servants were leading the way and setting the pace. They knew of my determination to reach Birnin Boko that day. In the late morning we rounded a bend and emerged on a straight road. In the distance we could see a town set on slightly raised ground. I knew this place. I had looked back at this town from this very point when I was being taken into slavery. I had not thought of this place for many years, but now my memories came back with such force that it seemed as if it was only yesterday that I had been here. My mind had built a bridge over those long, eventful years.

"Garin Bassam, that is it!" I shouted. My brain was flooded with a recollection of all the happenings in this place. This I knew was the town of Shehu Minchika, the great slave dealer. This was where I had been sold into slavery. Here Shehu Minchika ruled above the law, gathering children from the villages and selling them to faraway places.

Very clearly in my mind I saw the yard where I and other children had been kept like stray goats, to cry our eyes out. I remembered how Shehu Minchika had sent one of his men to whip us in that yard because of the noise of our weeping.

"You'd better save your tears for worse things ahead," he had said. And for many of those children no doubt a worse fate had lain ahead.

I told Fatima all that I remembered of the place and the people who lived in it. Soon we were riding through the streets of the town, attracting a lot of attention. I know now why this was. Most of the people here were poor. But even if a person was wealthy he dared not show it, for fear of being deprived of his wealth by Shehu Minchika. Only the sons of the Emir and the favoured among the nobles were allowed to own a horse. And these were few enough to be known. The rest of them who could afford to own and keep any beasts of burden therefore owned asses.

Four people, one of them a woman, on three horses were quite a sight and naturally attracted attention. We had ridden into the town to see it, but the town now turned out to see us. Shehu Minchika did not live in the heart of the town and could therefore not see us but he had many eyes from his followers who delighted in telling him all that they saw because he wanted to know and because they gained favour with him.

No sooner had we set foot in the town than his messengers told him of the four strangers, and he decided to invite us to his palace. He immediately sent two of his followers to present us with a small white calabash containing four big white kola nuts and to bid us welcome to Garin Bassam. Kolanuts were rare in those days and therefore very valuable and white kola nuts even more so. They were only given to people who were held in high esteem. The white calabash was meant to depict the status and friendliness of the giver. To accept this gift was to accept the invitation to pay a visit to the giver. Not to accept it was not only bad manners but an insult.

We were resting in the town centre, looking around us at the low round huts, the naked children, the stunted trees, when the messengers came. They came directly to me as the leader of our party. They squatted down on their heels as they delivered the message and handed over the gift. I accepted it readily.

I had many reasons for this. In the first place I did not want to offend Shehu Minchika who I knew was a ruthless man. I did not want to make an enemy of him. Secondly, I wanted to see this man whose reputation I knew well. I thought of him as the man to whom I had been sold like a goat, who had sent me cruelly into slavery and yet now sought my acquaintance. He would never guess that I had been one of the child- slaves herded into his yard many years ago.

I therefore eagerly agreed to meet this man, and we followed his messengers. As we went, my mind was filled with hate for the Shehu. He had done me much wrong. His agents had taken me from my home and sent me to years of slavery. The slavery might have lasted for many more years, perhaps forever, had fate not intervened. This man was the cause of much misery and sorrow in many homes, as he had been in mine.

Fatima seemed to sense my hatred. She drew close to me and placed her hand on my shoulder and she whispered: "Promise me you will do or say nothing rash. I can understand how you feel. But this is not the time to show resentment."

I nodded to show that I understood and agreed. We went on after that in silence and I had time to think how different my life would have been if this man had not lived or if he had pursued an honest trade like other people.

But then I might never have met Fatima and would have missed all the pleasure and joy which she had brought me. I knew from what I had heard that Shehu Minchika still bought and sold kidnapped children. I thought of the number of homes into which he had brought sorrow and the number of young men and young women who were scattered in strange countries slaving to make others rich. I remembered the young boys at that camp on the Sheik's plantation, living in silence and without hope. Something urged me to turn back and refuse to see him. I asked myself why I should give him honour where he deserved hatred and contempt. My first judgement prevailed however and I went on.

Fatima and I were ushered into Shehu Minchika's presence. What I saw shocked me. I think perhaps I had expected to see a great bearded figure dressed like a warrior because a man of his reputation should be a fighting man or a massive man sitting on a throne shouting orders to his followers and pronouncing harsh judgement on offenders.

But he was not like this. The Shehu was an old man who had dwindled with age into a small man. The only thing about him which had not shrunk was his turban which was golden in colour and huge in size. It seemed to weigh him down. He was bent and feeble and when he rose to receive us I had a strong inclination to crush him in my arms-and not for love or pity.

There was still about him that air of authority and power with which he had cloaked himself over the years. When he bade us welcome, the feebleness of the voice, by its sheer contrast to what I had expected, was bewildering. This man appeared like a ghost of his reputation. He was the picture of a failing champion. Except by the magic of his name, the memory of his past and the bounties of his wealth, how could this frail creature command such a huge following, loyalty and respect? But conscious of his own past, of his wealth and the indebtedness and fear of his followers, he could still act as the powerful man that he had been.

He seemed to be taking his time to gather himself to speak.......

The Shehu sat on beautifully coloured mats, supported by cushions covered with embroidered leather. He bade Fatima and me sit down next to him on the mat. This we did cross-legged, our hands in the hollow between our He seemed to be taking his time to gather himself to speak........ legs. We waited. He seemed to be taking time to gather himself to speak and I had a feeling that his mental faculties were failing with his physical ones.

"Welcome," he said at last. "Here in Garin Bassam we endeavour to make visitors to the town comfortable. We help them readily. Are you staying here or passing through?"

"We are on our way to Birnin Boko from the kingdom of Yelua. We wanted to see your town as we have heard so much of you. We are grateful for this chance of meeting you," I said.

This man could still smile. It was a smile of pride at his being known far afield to strangers. His smile illuminated the wrinkled face but did not improve it.

"So you have heard of me. Pray, what exactly have you heard?" he asked without making any effort at concealing his gràtification.

"Aren't you the famous Shehu Minchika, the generous noble who feeds thousands daily at his court, whose word is law, who is in fact, though not in name, the first citizen of this land, who can make and unmake, before whom thousands fall and hide their faces. Aren't you the same Shehu Minchika, the great slave dealer, the scourge of the towns and villages around, the provider of life to the great plantations of the desert border? He who has not heard of you has heard of no name."

This answer, which I gave to feed his vanity, pleased him immensely. He grinned foolishly and stroked his scanty grey beard and snapped his fingers.

Two servants came and knelt close to him and he whispered some words to them. They rose and left the room. In a short while they returned, each bearing a great brass tray. On one tray lay a long sword with a brass hilt, the blade encased in a leopard skin sheath. The sight of this sword called to my mind the sacred sword of my family which brought fame and honour to my grandfather and which was expected to bring me renown also. It reminded me also that it was still possible for me to win this renown even though I had abandoned hope of it when I was carried away into slavery. Now this same Minchika who had stood between me and the fulfillment of my father's dream was presenting me with a sword. A wicked thought crossed my mind and I said to myself: 'Perhaps someday I shall kill him with his own sword.'

This thought must have shown on my face, and, as if to warn me, Fatima nudged me. When I looked at her she smiled calmly into my eyes. I took the warning and smiled back at her and at everybody.

Meanwhile the Shehu stood up, took the sword by the blade and offered the hilt to me:

"A strong sword for a brave man; for you look to me a man among many. With this sword cut down your enemies and all who obstruct you. Revenge all wrongs done to you and to those whom you choose to help."

His words sounded to me like a curse on himself. This man was pronouncing a deadly sentence for himself with his own tongue. I smiled back at him as he expected but inside me I said a quiet: 'Amen,' to his prayer.

The Shehu had struck me at first as frail and helpless, but the longer I remained here the more I realised that though his frame was weak, his mind was still strong. Even now, I thought, this man enslaved helpless children and treated his followers with crushing harshness. To him, unless you were of noble rank, you were hardly any better than the rats that ate the corn in his barns.

After handing over the sword to me with all ceremony, he proceeded to honour my wife. The other tray contained a jar of sweet-smelling scent encased in beautifully worked leather.

"To the beautiful wife of a brave man," he said, as he handed the jar to Fatima who accepted it with grace and a smile. There was a noise of appreciation among those present and I knew that Fatima was again shedding her light and pleasantness to illuminate and warm the hearts of these people.

Shehu Minchika returned to his seat among the cushions and seemed lost in them except for the glitter of his huge turban. He seemed to be waiting for something and I knew what was expected of me. He had played his own part in the drama of exchanging gifts and was waiting for me to respond. I was not prepared for this because all that I had I owed to Al Atiku's charity. But I had to do something quickly or lose all the respect so far given me. I had to think very fast and sort out mentally the various objects presented to me by Al Atiku. I could not think fast enough. But I was saved by Fatima.

"The Fez cap," she whispered.

"Yes, the Fez cap," I agreed. I looked at her and she read in my eyes the gratitude to a most intelligent and helpful wife.

I hailed one of the servants who had come with us and whispered my instruction to him. Soon he was back with the Fez cap wrapped as it was presented to me. As I handed it to the Shehu, I said: "I give this to him who obeys no man, over whom no one but Allah has control." He was again elated.

When this ceremony was over I said to him: "It would give me great pleasure to see the extent of your palace." I was intent on seeing again that yard where we were quartered like goats on the day after my capture. I wanted to see the scene of my childhood misery and to see if it was still used for the same diabolical purpose.

This man was inordinately vain. He rose instantly and led the way. Fatima came with me but the peculiar twist of her mouth seemed to hint at my folly in making this trip round. To Fatima my mind was like a book. She read one thought after the other. I only had to turn the page.

We went from one apartment to another and the feeble voice of our host told the story of everything and every place. I feigned immense interest though I was interested in only one place: the yard. We went everywhere except to that yard and I wondered if it was still there.

Then as we passed by a long mud wall I thought I heard someone sobbing. At the same time I saw Fatima straighten up and I was in no doubt she too had heard. Someone behind that wall was wailing and that knowledge was enough for me. It was all the evidence that I needed. Shehu Minchika still carried on the accursed trade. He had wealth and all the power that money could buy, all the power that went with money in a primitive society, yet he still traded in human beings, destroying the peace and love of simple folks in their lowly homes.

Why did he do it? After hearing that sobbing, I had no doubt that it was the same yard where I had cried as a child. I wondered if he heard the wailing because he did not seem to notice it. Perhaps he was so used to it that it meant nothing to him. I thought I would embarrass him by asking a forthright question:

"I think I hear someone crying behind the walls," I said looking him straight in the eye. "My palace is a small world," he said. "In it live people of diverse nature and moods. Some are happy and others are sad. While some laugh, others weep.

I have lived with all sorts of men for too long to care about what ails them and what gladdens their hearts. Those you hear are young children who have been sold to me as slaves."

"Then they cry because they don't like it," I answered.

"That must be so. I guess slavery is not a pleasant experience, but I am sure it cannot all be bad," he said.

"Why do you think so?" I asked.

"Because oftentimes some of them are lucky and have kind masters and they are treated like children of their masters. They then lead a happier life than they were used to or than they would ever have lived. Many slaves are better off than the people who flock around this palace or than many people in the poor villages."

I knew that, even though I would not accept his theory, this reasoning was correct. If I hadn't been taken into slavery I would not have become the sort of person who could stand up to him now. But I knew that my case was an exception. Many slaves lived and died in drudgery and degradation. He seemed to be justifying his wickedness and felt no remorse for the wrongs he was doing, and I hated him. But I decided to pursue this matter further: "Don't you ever think how unhappy many of these children are away from home?" I asked.

"The unhappiness will soon pass. Children have very short memories. They soon forget their home and the life they have lived and absorbed into the new one. They form new friendships and soon are grateful for being taken away from home. That is why it is better to have them while young. Older ones tend to be more difficult," he answered.

"But, what about the family from which the child is stolen?" I asked.

"You call it 'stolen' as if it were a sin. I trade in slaves as any other man will trade in sheep. I do not go into the homes to take the children. I only buy cheap and sell 'dear' and keep the difference. I do not concern myself about the homes. The world is filled with bad luck and unhappiness. This is their share of it. I have mine, you have yours. I do not keep these slaves. I do not need them. Have you seen the hundreds of my followers who enslave themselves to me? If the parents of these enslaved children were to live in this town, I am sure that many of them would be like these others and give away their children to me." Shehu Minchika was not making any real effort to convince me of the rightness of his deeds. He was simply telling me how he saw the whole thing and his logic was not bad either.

Yet to agree with him was to support a wrong because a good reason had been found for it. Slavery was wrong, is wrong and will ever be wrong. I pressed him further: "You are an old man now; when you depart from here, I suppose there will be an end to the trade in kidnapped children," I said.

"Oh no! I have children who are going to step into my shoes. They will continue my life's work. They are in the business already and grow rich in it," he answered.

'So this wickedness will continue in order to keep this family wealthy,' I thought to myself. 'This must stop and I am going to help in stopping it, if it is the only good thing I ever do. A child born into a family has a right to live and grow up in that family. Parents have a right to the joy of having children growing up around them. Whoever interferes with this joy is an enemy of mankind and deserves no mercy.'

I was tempted to tell Shehu all this and me more, but the look on Fatima's face stopped me. Her meaning was clear; she was warning me no to be rash. I did nothing rash; I said nothing further, but my silence and the questions I had asked made the Shehu uneasy. He too was silent and the atmosphere grew tense. From what we had said the clash of ideas between us was now evident. All the pretended cordiality was gone and the cold heavy hand of dislike was falling on both of us.

Discretion however stopped us both from the open demonstration of this feeling. We turned to go back to the hall. He still had enough courage and self-control as we passed the gate which led into the yard to ask if I would take a look into the yard. I declined and for this I had many reasons. I did not want to see wretched children whom I could do nothing to assist. I knew that the sight of them might force me to say things which were better not said while I had no means of defending myself. We were not invited to stay longer and we parted outside the hall where much honour had been lavished on us earlier. The parting was cold and stiff. I remember my parting words:

"We shall meet again.

He seemed to understand my meaning and nodded his head as if accepting a challenge.

4. Home

We sped out of the town as if running from a plagued city. We did not look back. We did not speak. The servants had not toured the palace with us and did not witness the change from cordiality to frigidity. So they must have been surprised to see our sudden departure and the absence of friendliness. Whatever they felt, they kept their own counsel.

Fatima sat close to me and I did not know how to interpret her silence. It could be evidence of her disappointment in me for not having enough wit to handle the situation better in spite of her warning and promptings. It could also be that she understood and sympathized with my inability to control my emotions as I controlled my mouth. She did not speak until I asked over my shoulder how she was feeling:

"Fine!" She spoke sharply almost before I had asked the question. I still did not understand her. After going some distance, I thought it was time we had something to eat and I said so.

"Yes!" she answered.

These answers in one syllable gave no indication of what went on in her mind. When I helped her down from the horse, she straightened up to look into my face. "Shettima," she said, "you have a kind heart and you are brave. But you are not very discreet. All the same I am proud of you."

This was a great relief for me. Already I had come to regard Fatima as a guardian angel, who knew right from wrong and would ensure success to a project once she gave it her blessing. I now had something to live and work for. I had accepted as a mission the task of putting an end to the wicked trafficking in human beings. But, we had lost much time in Garin Bassam; and now we were on our way home again to Birnin Boko. No preparations would be made against my coming. But I had no doubt that the hearts and hearths there would be warm even though the bare mud floor would be hard and cold.

I speculated on the changes that would have taken place since I left: my sisters grown up, my mother on the verge of old age. Yet I knew that time and age would not touch my mother. She would be too strong for them. I wondered if there would be many in the village who would remember the small boy who was taken away. I did not worry about what Fatima would think of our small house. I had enough faith in her to know that she would understand and make the most of what was available.

I did not worry either about her acceptance by the family; she was not only my beloved wife, but also a woman of rare beauty and character.

I wanted to reach home before dark, so we galloped fast along the narrow path. It was nearing dark before I began to feel that the country around me had a childhood familiarity. Then I had that strange feeling of home-coming which is in the main pleasant and sweet but nevertheless leaves a sour taste in the mouth. I knew that soon we would come to the sleepy village of Birnin Boko which was my family home, where I would be loved and respected, but where I could only be a big man in a small place.

As I approached the village I realised that no one can stay the hand of fate. Who could have thought on the day I was kidnapped that I would once again come to this village? Other mothers would have been relieved that it was not their son who was kidnapped. They would certainly have warned their children not to go alone into the bush or they would suffer my fate. But now, I was back in the village, more cultured, more learned than any of those who were children when I was a child. I was returning with a beautiful and intelligent wife. What would people think of us? Would they honour me for turning slavery into victory and success? Would they be happy at my coming and not be jealous of my achievements? Look at me! I wore the garments which Al Atiku gave me, I rode a horse, I spoke many different tongues, I saw many people and places.

We rode into the village, four of us and three horses. One horse and rider would have been quite a sight in this village. It would have drawn the children out running and jumping behind the horse, shouting and clapping after it.

It would have made the older people peep through the doors and crane their necks in order to get a glance. Three horses and four riders including a woman would awaken many emotions in the minds of these people: pleasure, surprise and fear. Some would withdraw into the recesses of their dark rooms, while some would wish to see more and understand. I was not surprised then to see that, while the children at first hesitantly and then gleefully followed us, some older people who were outside rose up and slipped into their houses, while some who had been inside came to their doors to stand and stare.

My home was at the far end of the village. As we rode through the village I was conscious of the many pairs of inquisitive eyes that followed us. That we did not stop to ask our way further increased their curiosity. Now I saw our house. A young woman stood outside, shading her eyes with her hand. No doubt she wanted to see more clearly the strange sight before her. I knew it was Halima: I knew her poise, her solid frame like my mother's and the slight inclination of her proud head.

As we approached I could tell the moment at which she recognised me. She did not seem to be surprised that it was I. She did not even wait to ascertain that her guess was correct. She threw away the basket which she was holding and ran towards us. She called out: "Shettima! You are back! I have waited for so long!"

Then she started to weep. I jumped down from the horse and held her close to my chest. She rested there as if she was accustomed to do so. Now I was grown tall and broad, no longer the little child who used to lie face downwards on her own chest. She seemed to have seen me grow through the years and accepted the great change in me. I looked up at Fatima as she sat on the horse, fearing she might be jealous of the degree of love between Halima and me.

"Shettima! You are back! I have waited for so long."

But she smiled and nodded her understanding. "Shettima! You are back! I have waited for so long."

A crowd gathered round us. Then I saw that among the crowd watching the reunion drama with my mother. She stood there composed, her arms folded across her chest, on her face patience and eagerness, relief and gratitude. She waited for my sister to finish venting her great emotion and to leave the stage for her.

If I had not gently pushed away my sister, we would have been standing there for many hours. I moved near my mother and with one hand, as Halima still held onto the other, drew her to me and hugged her.

At first I thought that she was cold but when she folded her arms around my neck, compelling Halima to release me, and shed tears of joy, I discovered many things about her. Beneath her almost masculine facade was feminine softness and weakness. I had no doubt about my mother's love for me and that the years I had been gone had been for her one long period of anguish and sorrow. The crowd stood in silence. No one spoke as if it was forbidden to violate the sacredness of this moment. Then my mother spoke: "So, Gattam was right," she said. "Gattam, my husband! I shall never cease to honour your memory! You have brought back our son. Your frame was weak but which man could do better than you have done!"

Here again was another side of this unique woman, my mother. She had loved, and adored, and honoured her husband like any woman; though she was so strong and he so frail.

But I had not come back alone and Fatima was being left out of our reunion. As usual she came to my aid. When I turned around she was standing behind me. The people around were now gazing on Fatima as if she had not been there before but had suddenly appeared on the scene. Indeed the people had every excuse for regarding her so curiously.

Fatima was different from any woman there. She stood there like one of the goddesses we read about in ancient books, as if she had come down from heaven to dwell among mortals. She was taller than every other woman and slender. The manner and quality of her dress added to her dignity. But there was something extra in her looks and in her carriage that compelled admiration and awe. If Fatima had been in rags or naked from the waist upward like the other women who now stood in silence, she would still be different, she would still compel admiration and reverence.

"Will you not introduce me to your mother, Shettima?" Fatima asked, smiling. She spoke in Arabic and it was now that I realised that I had been addressed all the time in my native language and I had understood everything. It had come to me naturally and ten years' absence had not made any difference. Fatima must now learn our language if she were to join our family fully.

"Mother, this is my wife," I said, wondering if my mother would accept her as a daughter and not see her as a rival and a stranger.

"You are welcome," said my mother. Her arms stretched wide open in an invitation to Fatima to squeeze herself into the comfort, protection and warmth which she would give her:

"Anyone whom my son loves, I love; anyone who loves my son loves me. If you are my son's wife then this is your home and I am your mother. I don't know where you came from or who you are, but all we have to offer is yours. We may be rough but we are real. If you accept us as we now accept you, you will have from us that which is more than wealth. You will have our love."

I knew what this welcome must mean to Fatima. She had not known her mother's love. Fatima, as I have said, was enslaved while she was too young to retain the memory of her childhood. It was the first time she had had the chance of knowing a mother's love. This was too much kindness and Fatima, from whom neither the pain of punishment nor the disgrace of slavery had drawn a tear, wept tears of joy. It required the warmth of my arms around her and the whispers of my love into her ear to comfort her.

My mother did not wish the crowd standing round to witness this show of emotion, so she led Fatima gently inside. My sister and I followed and the silent crowd took our departure as a signal to start talking. Their voices reached my ears inside the house. The family, my mother, my sister, my wife and I, were now gathered in the house and the centre of all the attention was Fatima. While my mother was fussing over getting ready water for Fatima to have her bath, my sister was preparing the rope-sponge and fetching the soap, removing her shoes and guiding her to the bamboo shed behind the house for her bath.

This was a true home-coming. Could anything be dearer? It was poor in its surroundings; but it was rich, very rich, in love and sincerity. Beside it, the wealth and greatness of Sheik Maitama's empire paled into insignificance. All that the Sheik owned and all the power he could wield, could not substitute for this small but great institution-the home.

This was Fatima's first contact with a real home and she was overwhelmed with the contentment, the love, the openness, the simplicity and sincerity. Every action, she discovered, arose from the heart without the hope of reward or praise. There was no attempt to hide anything because it was not good enough. From where she sat, Fatima could see almost every part of the small house, yet she felt that there was so much love in it that it could fill and overflow the palaces of Shehu Minchika or of Sheik Maitama.

Into this home I settled with Fatima. Both the home and the village quickly accepted me and my bride. Fatima got over the language barrier quickly for there were many eager teachers and she was an anxious learner. Even little children delighted to speak to her and took much pleasure in being able to help her to learn. I was however her most present and ready teacher. It was fun for both of us, everywhere and at all times.

5. Life in Birnin Boko

Quickly Fatima became the idol of the village women. She seemed to have cast her spell on all, young and old, and they were drawn closely to her. She made herself available to them all and the men, husbands and fathers did nothing to stop them spending their time with her.

When Fatima had been a slave she had lived in the palace of the Sheik and had become used to a life that meant comfort and ease. For a short time she had had to accept the change in her fortune to toil in squalor in atonement for her sin of loving me. But most of her life had been lived in a rich setting. Yet she fitted into our home in Birnin Boko as if she had been born there.

Because Fatima was so occupied with the village women, I found time lying heavily on my hands. At first, all I wanted to do was to go round and round the village talking to the men about old times, about my experience and life in any, a foreign land, about the pains and, if pleasures of slavery, about the things I had learnt and the people I had met. I told them of my luck in being favoured by the Sheik's son and the exploits that led to my being set free.

There was soon no doubt in my mind that they thought of me as a hero. Heroes, they agreed, are born and not made, and when they heard how as a child I had dared to attack the wicked Matamba, overseer of the Sheik's field workers, and rescue my helpless friend, Al Atiku, they thought I must be a hero-born. When they heard of my escape and Al Atiku's pursuit, they asked who would surrender himself to an enemy because he was also a friend? They thought that only a born hero could have turned disaster into success at the last minute.

I thought I had told them the stories of my various adventures without embellishment. I was therefore surprised when scraps of these stories came back to me very highly distorted and exaggerated. I had never said anything that might give anyone the impression that I was a warrior. I had no better claim to this title than any of them who had listened to me, but by a curious twist of their minds they had cloaked me with the qualities of a hero and a warrior. It was to them a natural development, warriors like heroes, are born. The grandson of a famous warrior must be a warrior. So, without having fought a battle or even wielded the famous family sword, I had won renown.

And yet I had hardly touched the sword. On the day I arrived, Halima had handed the sword and the family seal over to me with the last message of my late father. I had held the sword and tried to use it on an invisible foe. Halima had gazed into my face as if expecting to see a transformation in fulfillment of the belief that at the touch of the sword, the spirit of my great ancestor would descend on me. I had smiled at her and she had deluded herself into seeing some light in my face as if the touch of the sword had brought with it the light of the guardian spirit.

The village was satisfied that in the event of a war, a very remote possibility even in those days, a leader was at hand. All the young men on their minds to serve under me should war ever come. I knew next to nothing about fighting a battle or how to organise a fighting army, however small. But I took my solace in the knowledge that no war was likely to break out between these peace-loving people and their equally peace-loving neighbours.

The young men of Birnin Boko soon wanted to learn horse riding. One after the other and sometimes in groups of three or four, they came to me and begged to be taught to ride. I was eager to teach them but I was reluctant to use my own horse. I was able to make them see how important my horse was to me and that I could not, much as I wanted to teach them, have inexperienced riders ruining it. We agreed on a scheme which would make riding lessons possible. They would each contribute money to buy horses for themselves.

I was surprised at the rate at which the money was raised. The idea became an obsession among the men. Even the younger boys caught it. Age-groups vied with each other about the number of horses they would have. I was alarmed because this trend threatened to

change the face of the village, but I also could
see that it could be a healthy thing. The young
men were working and training together and
learning a new skill.

The horses were brought to the village
from the horse market further north in groups
and it was a hard job for me to break them in
and teach the men. But I worked hard and soon
had some of the best students helping me. I
taught them how to look after the horses and
how to get the best out of them. In no time the
dull and sleepy village had become wakeful and
active. Feeding and caring for the horses took
time and absorbed the idle moments of the
young men. It did, in some cases, provide for
the younger boys an opportunity of making
some money. They -fetched the water, bathed
the horses, and cut the grass for their fodder. It
provided entertainment for the women, old men

and the little children as the men soon delighted in showing off their growing prowess.

News of the doings in Birnin Boko spread to neighbouring villages and towns and stories were built around me. Poor as I was, the people both in Birnin Boko and the other villages had come to believe that I was rich, that I had amassed a lot of wealth in the course of my sojourn in strange countries.

It went round that I was the head of the cavalry of the Sultan of Yelua, the voice of the desert, and that I had led the Sultan's army many successful battles and that any time the Sultan was again in trouble I would surely be sent for.

They had built up stories about Fatima, too. She was, the story went, the daughter of a great and wealthy Sheik who, on account of his daughter's love for me, had bought me my freedom and had given us enough money to last us all our lives. They set my wife's beauty, her manners and comportment down to her noble birth and upbringing.

They thought of me as a hero and in everything I did, they saw heroism. When I spoke or rode or walked, they saw the style of the hero in it. There was nothing I could do to dispel this image. Even my mother and my sister shared in this hero-worshipping.

They saw in me now a fulfillment of all their past dreams. They saw a fulfillment of the hopes and desires of my father who, though weak and frail himself, had ambitions through me, his only son. Fatima understood my plight and was always ready to help me fulfill many of the obligations which my supposed nobility now imposed. She herself had such natural nobility that her everyday behaviour seemed to

the village people the behaviour of a noble's
daughter.

Both Fatima and I made no conscious
effort to encourage them in this wrong notion,
but there was little we could do to discourage
them. What was ordinary to us was by their
standards out of the ordinary. They saw
something lofty in everything we did or said.
Our clothes, which we received as gifts from
our master and mistress, were, to them, very
grand. The little sum of money we had went a
long way since living in the village was very
inexpensive. Even living in the lowly hut was
seen as an act of heroism for humility is a mark
of true heroism. If we wanted a palace, they
believed, we could have built one since we had
the means.

This quality of humility did not suffer
any damage when because of the need for more
space I decided to extend our house. I told no

one about this even though according to custom, I was, like any other young man entitled to free communal labour in building a house. Since my return, I have joined on two occasions in giving such free labour. I could have built the extension by myself. But on the day that I started to dig the ground, it was known and once again my heroism was confirmed because a hero does not impose himself on others. Help came quickly and in a short time the extension was completed.

6. Trouble at Garin Bassam

Now let me go back to tell you about the
two servants of my friend Al Atiku, who had
accompanied us back to Birnin Boko. It is their
tale which leads us on to my own further
adventures. We had for some time
accommodated them as comfortably as possible
in our small house. They had indeed stayed to
help me with the breaking of the first horses,
and it was only when they saw me well settled
that they returned to their master.

On the day of their departure both
Fatima and I left Birnin Boko with them and,
after travelling for about an hour, bade them
Godspeed and goodbye. They were to convey to
Al Atiku and Sherifat and others our good
wishes and news of our new life. We turned
back and made for home in a leisurely manner.

We speculated on how soon these men would reach Yelua, for we never thought that grown men would meet any mishap on the way.

A short time after we parted with them we met a man on an ass going along the road in their direction. We spared no thought for him after exchanging the normal traveller's greetings. We had seen him in the village for some time past and had understood he was a travelling trader. It was much later that we learnt the truth about this man. He was in fact a spy in the service of Shehu Minchika of Garin Bassam.

He had arrived in Birnin Boko shortly after our return. Because of the commotion which followed our arrival in Birnin Boko, his arrival attracted little notice. He had stayed quietly in the village doing some petty trading. We learnt later that he had been sent after us by Shehu Minchika who, after our unpleasant parting, wanted to keep track of us, to know what possible source of danger and trouble to him I might constitute.

In the village he successfully presumed on the hospitality of the people. He was taken in as a travelling trader who needed rest and time to recover from a sudden illness. No one doubted his story and much sympathy and care were lavished on him. His coming was not strange and it aroused no suspicion. The many questions which he asked about me seemed natural to the villagers at that time. When he moved round the village slowly like a convalescent, the people gave him pity and ready answers to his questions. He soon learnt all that he wanted to know. Even when, on the day that the servants left on their return journey, he suddenly decided to leave and suddenly seemed fully recovered, the people just felt pleased for him. They did not connect his departure even remotely with the departure of the servants. So, too, when the servants, who were riding at a leisurely pace, were overtaken by this man who gave them a smile as he hurried by, they thought nothing of it. If only they had known what his mission was they would have cursed the treachery of man!

They planned to bypass Garin Bassam as they had seen enough of this place on their outward journey and there was no need to tarry there again. So they made straight for the route that led to the desert.

They had hardly taken the first bend away from Garin Bassam when they saw before them a group of about twelve men barring the way. Each carried a long spear. The two servants did not at first understand the meaning of this and did not think that it had anything to do with them.

They carried no treasure which could attract bandits; they had not trespassed and they had wounded nobody's pride. But how little they knew about the workings of the mind and the high-handedness of Shehu Minchika! He hardly ever concerned himself with the rights or wrongs of a course of action as long as it served his purpose. Since there was no one to challenge his power he did as he pleased.

So with no fear of danger the two servants rode on towards these men. The group began to move towards them, pressed together, holding their spears in position for action. This did not frighten the servants who felt that this action could not be directed against them, since it was too elaborate and too cautious for dealing with two unarmed men. They were therefore astonished when, as they met, some of the men seized their horses' bridles, while others poised their spears as if to strike.

It was an amateurish show which encouraged the two men to challenge them. While the spear-bearers were dancing round them, the two servants, who were still on their horses, struck at the men beside them and spurred their horses. The horses responded with a violent plunge which threw the men holding them to the ground. The horses made off leaving the men sprawling on the grass while the spear-men stood too dazed to move.

Slowly the 'soldiers of Minchika' rose from the ground to shake the dust and leaves from their scanty clothes. They returned home with their 'wounds of war' to tell an exaggerated story of a fierce encounter with the two armed horsemen who had been rein- forced by about fifteen others who had been in hiding. The Shehu was indignant and blamed me for this defeat of his 'warriors'. He was determined to this shame on anyone who was avenge connected, no matter how remotely, with the two horsemen.

The horses responded with a violent plunge which threw the man holding them to the ground.

Like all vain persons he was sure that he could deal with anyone who challenged him. He had not enough modesty and sense to realise that men who carried long spears were not necessarily good soldiers and number was not an advantage unless it was backed by skill and courage. Soldiers needed good leadership and a good cause to fight for. Shehu Minchika's 'soldiers' lacked both.

The two servants reached the place of Sheik Maitama and there told Al Atiku, their master of the great reception accorded me and Fatima, and the kindness of the people of Birnin Boko and their encounter and defeat of the 'soldiers of Minchika'. The story of the encounter as it was told at first amused Al Atiku, but later, when he got over the ludicrous side of it, he wondered why it was necessary for Shehu Minchika to trouble his men. The more he thought of it the less he liked it.

Al Atiku believed that excessive use of power must be discouraged everywhere. All men, whether they are slaves, servants or free men, had the right to go untroubled on their journeys. All men, he believed, have their longings and hopes however little and unworthy. So long therefore as they did not trouble anyone they had a right to serve, labour and live in peace. Like me, Al Atiku, without ever meeting Shehu Minchika had, from what he had heard of him, set him down as an enemy of mankind. He had often felt that he would like to do something about him.

Shehu Minchika, the terror of Garin Bassam and the powerful slave dealer, was gaining in years and gaining more enemies even as he was losing his strength, health and his hold on his followers. Now, though he did not know it, he was threatened on one side by Al Atiku and the host of people who served the

Sheik and loved and respected him, and on the other by me, Shettima, son of Gattama Boko, and all the horse-riding Birnin Boko men who loved and respected me. On the other hand Shehu Minchika himself was the master of time- serving, lazy and cowardly parasites and flatterers. They loved Shehu Minchika's gifts but not him, more so now that he could not shout as loudly as before and therefore frightened them less.

Al Atiku and I, each unaware of the other's feeling of hostility towards the Shehu, waited for an excuse to strike at him. Al Atiku could raise a small fighting army, and he was quite sure from the report he got from his two servants that any opposition which the Shehu could raise would be undisciplined, ragged and unskilled. I, on the other hand, knew little about the Shehu's fighting force but I knew two useful things. In the first place, the Shehu had never won renown as a soldier and leader of an army. In the second place, I now had devoted young men who were learning to play any trick with their horses, who were amenable to discipline and had a cause to fight for. The odds were against the Shehu and, unknown to him, he now had two real enemies.

In the past Shehu Minchika had wielded much power in his domain. Now he thought, why not make this power felt beyond it? How else could he demonstrate his dying power and feed his senile vanity other than by looking for fresh conquests further afield? He did not really want to fight to subjugate anyone beyond his domain but he wanted recognition and fame. He wanted important people in faraway places to acknowledge that there was a greater man elsewhere. He wanted them to speak his name, Shehu Minchika; to know of his town, Garin Bassam; to fear his followers, numbered in thousands; and to recognise his claim to fame as the greatest slave dealer and the terror of the land. His vanity had blinded him to the dangers and follies of his planned excesses. He thought only of the fame his action could attract and nothing at all of the dangers to which he would expose himself. It is not surprising therefore that he provided the needed excuse for each of his potential enemies to descend upon him with fury.

The labour force in Sheik Maitama's establishment often needed replenishment and reinforcement. The business was expanding fast, some slaves were getting too old for active work; a few had done their twenty years' service and gained their freedom. More slaves must be bought and the most fertile and surest source was, of course, Garin Bassam. The Sheik was an old customer of the Shehu though they had never met, and neither knew much more about the other than that one was a great buyer and the other a great seller of slaves.

Each was important in his own right and in his own domain. There had never been, and there was no need for, any comparison of their wealth, strength and importance. And there might never have been any clash and the need to test the strength of one against the other if Shehu Minchika had been able to contain his vanity and had not decided to spread his fame far afield or drum the fact of his greatness into the ears of the high and lowly no matter how distant. He did not care what means and antics he employed so long as he gained the end which he desired. Something was urging him blindly on to his doom.

A few short months after the meeting outside Garin Bassam, the Sheik's servants were ready to go on their journey to buy slaves as usual. Al Atiku heard about this and saw that there was the opportunity to bring to the Shehu's notice, as he surely did not know, whose servants it was that he had so brutally assaulted and to extract some kind of apology for the attack. The Shehu's act was wrong, but it might be forgiven if he could plead ignorance of whose servants those two were. In that case he would not be guilty of an affront to Sheik Maitama, the Lion of the Desert, and there might be no excuse to get even with him. Al Atiku therefore gave the Sheik's servants orders to tell the Shehu of the displeasure of the Sheik at the attack on his two servants.

When the Sheik's servants arrived in Garin Bassam, they were accorded the usual courtesy and hospitality. Bargains were struck, the necessary payments made and everybody was happy about the business except the unhappy children who were being sold. Then the Sheik's servants thought it was time to give the Shehu the message from Al Atiku:

"Our lord and master, Sheik Maitama, the Lion of the Desert, your customer and friend, complained that two of his servants were returning from Birnin Boko some time ago and were assaulted by your men," they told the Shehu. "He thought you probably did not know that they were his servants or you would not have attacked them."

"Ah!" shouted Shehu Minchika. "So it was your lord and master who sent an army to attack my men who were peacefully patrolling the area! Now I have the clue I wanted and I know whom I have to deal with and who must pay for the affront.

I knew that they were returning from Birnin Boko where they had gone with that slave they called Shettima," he went on. "I might have dealt with Shettima, sacked the whole village of Birnin Boko and taken all of them as slaves, but I was in no hurry until now. Now the time has come when I have to deal with them."

He was very excited and he seemed to be straining himself to make his feeble voice strong and awe-inspiring. The visitors were surprised at his words. They had expected the ordinary courtesy of an expression of regret and apology for annoying the servants of a friend. The matter could then have rested there. They had not expected to hear this excited declaration against their master and his friend, Shettima. But they had not yet heard or seen the worst.

Shehu Minchika called four of his servants to him and ordered them:

"Arrest these two men and lock them up to await my pleasure. Return the young slaves to the yard and sell them over again." The men were immediately seized. They did not resist since they knew it would be futile to do so. But before they were led away they made a request: "Kindly send a messenger to tell our companions to take the news of our arrest home so that our master may arrange to pay you a handsome ransom.

"So you have a bodyguard somewhere and you want to get my messengers trapped?" the Shehu shrieked at them. "There are only two of them. Surely they cannot do much harm to your valiant soldiers," said the captives, hoping to calm the old man."Indeed they cannot. I shall send four of my bravest soldiers. I like the idea of your master paying me a ransom. He will, on the one hand, pay for the sins of his servants and, on the other, acknowledge my superiority."

So Shehu Minchika dispatched four of his men on foot armed with spears. When the

Sheik's men heard his message they were furious. They were experienced and trained fighters and they drew their swords to fight the Shehu's men. It was a one-sided fight with the Sheik's men overcoming the Shehu's soldiers with remarkable ease and capturing three of them. The other one dropped his spear for dear life with blood pouring down his cheek. He stammered out the story of a brave fight in which they had been out-numbered by nine armed horsemen. He told of the capture of his three companions and his own heroic escape.

The Shehu asked for his drink of drugged 'fura', which served him like an opiate in such situations, giving him unusual courage and deadening his senses against pain and fear. He ordered a troop of fifteen men to go after the Sheik's men and bring them back as captives. He ordered the two men whom he had locked up to be brought out to him in chains: "I am wondering what I should do to punish you," he said. "I have thought of slashing off your ears, of pulling off the nails of your fingers and toes, of knocking out some of your teeth and of tying you to a tree to be beaten to death. I do not think any of these punishments are severe enough. There are only two of you. I would rather have a whole host of your Sheik's soldiers suffering before me at the same time. Perhaps your Sheik will suffer with them too. So, go back into the cell and wait for your end," he concluded.

7. War with the Shehu

When the men had been led away, the Shehu called to him two other messengers and gave them orders:

"Get two asses and ride fast to Birnin Boko. Seek out the ex-slave they call Shettima and tell him this: 'Shehu Minchika, the terror of Garin Bassam, bids him come here with his wife and his horsemen and surrender themselves or else he will descend on Birnin Boko and take every man, woman and child to be sold into slavery in distant lands.'"

The messengers came to Birnin Boko and gave me the Shehu's message. It made me laugh. In the first place, I knew that the Shehu did not have the soldiers to fight a battle. In the second place, I did not know what prompted this mad declaration of war which I knew I could win easily even with only twenty men.

From the messengers, however, who showed every sign of fear and would do anything to be allowed to return free and unhurt, I learnt the story of the attack on Al Atiku's two servants. I learnt also of the arrest of the Sheik's slave buyers and the encounter with their companions.

So I called the young men of the village round and asked the messengers to repeat their story. After a short conference with my men, I sent this message back to Shehu Minchika: "Your cup of iniquities is full and by the grace of Allah, you will drink the last drop of it in less than twenty-four hours from now. I am on my way to Garin Bassam and the devil takes any man who opposes me."

Then I dismissed the messengers and, from the many volunteers among the young men, I chose only twenty-five to accompany me to Garin Bassam. Each mounted his horse carrying a leather shield and a sharp sword or cutlass.

These few men made up my army but it was a formidable army in comparison to the spear- carrying rabble which the Shehu would gather. In a few hours' time I and my army left Birnin Boko with the blessings of our wives and mothers and the applause of the whole village. I carried the sword of my famous grandfather; everybody thought the spirit of my grandfather was upon me and victory was sure. My mother with pride watched and wished my father were alive to see the fulfillment of his dream. Here was a son of Gattama to wield the sword and to win renown! Halima ran in and brought me the seal, to protect my life and to defend me from danger.

Fatima showed no weakness for she did not believe that any harm would come to me. I was brave, strong and clever. I was chosen by Allah to lead my people and to put an end to the misery caused to parents and children.

We went, twenty-six brave soldiers, with a cause to fight. We went at first trotting and later galloping towards Garin Bassam to face the Shehu's 'army' that had neither courage nor a belief in what they were fighting for. They had hardly anything to gain if they won, for the Shehu would claim all the glory and the benefit.

I had yet another reason for undertaking this expedition. By assaulting and manhandling Sheik Maitama's men, Shehu Minchika had shown that he had no regard for anyone. For the wrongs done to my friends, the Sheik and his son Al Atiku, I felt myself bound to punish the Shehu and put him in a place from where he could give no offence to anyone ever again. Sol led my men, fortified by this sense of duty and justice.

When his messengers returned to the Shehu with my harsh reply, he summoned his men and ordered them to arm themselves with their spears to go to Birnin B.oko and bring me bound hand and foot. They were also to bring back as many men, women and children as they could. He told them that it was going to be an easy task for no one could stand against Shehu Minchika the great slave dealer.

The men obeyed but they had their doubts. Each believed within himself that it was not worth his while to risk his life. Each would use the slightest opportunity to escape danger. They all saw the needlessness of the strife which Shehu Minchika had of late engaged in and doubted his sanity. Some saw in it all the approach of an ignoble end to his life - a life which had been a record of atrocity, vanity and heartlessness.

They set out for Birnin Boko, about a hundred strong. They went on foot and never was there a motley crowd of spineless individuals set on a most risky adventure, in slavish obedience to orders from a weakling whose only power was in the wealth he had amassed and the regular food he provided his followers.

The rabble went on; each dressed only in a leather kilt. They had the build of soldiers: tall, muscular, heads clean shaven and black. If wild looks and unkempt beards were assets in warfare they might have proved formidable. But as it was and always is, strength, discipline, training, skill and intelligence are the factors that spell victory. These were as wanting in this rabble as they were abundant in my little army.

I had sent ahead an intelligent young man to scout round and hurry back with the news as soon as he sighted the enemy. The rest had taken shelter under a shea-butter tree to refresh themselves and to remind themselves of the moves in response to orders from me. They seemed no more excited than they would have been if they were going on a hunting expedition.

Soon we saw the scout galloping towards us and we knew that he had news for us. He told us of the crowd of spear-men. It was not more than I had expected and I was sure I and my men could deal with them.

We all mounted and I quickly moved my men forward to a spot where the bush could provide us some cover. The party split into two and each part took cover on one side of the narrow road. The men stood ready, spaced out on their horses. They waited silently for the enemy and my order.

The Shehu's crowd came, talking loudly and marching along in a disorderly manner. They seemed to believe that the sight of them alone would defeat the enemy. No one seemed to be leading. They were in no way prepared for a surprise.

They were within yards of our hiding place when I gave a light whistle. This was the agreed signal to warn the men to get ready for the next order. The Shehu's crowd was talking too much to hear this whistle and straggled on carrying their spears awkwardly and presenting an easy target.

"Attack!" I cried. And in the next few minutes a scene was staged which was both ludicrous and tragic. Horsemen with shining cutlasses rushed from all sides upon the cluster of untrained men. They fell before the horses, wounding one another with their long awkward spears. They put up no fight at all, too terrified to know what to do. What was uppermost in their minds was how to escape without fighting. They threw away their spears and as many as could avoid the heavy hooves of the horses and the blades of the swords made for the bush. Those who were too hurt to run and those whose lines of escape were barred knelt down, raising their hands in a plea for mercy.

I was not after their blood for I knew that they were only obeying the wicked orders of their master. I left a few horsemen to round up these disarmed 'soldiers' and ordered the rest to pursue and bring back the fleeing ones. This took no time and as many as could be found were brought back. Not more than ten escaped. A few were killed, but many were wounded. Those who were not wounded were roped together and made to sit on the grass. Four of my horsemen were left to look after them.

I and the remaining horsemen went at a great speed towards Garin Bassam to the palace of Shehu Minchika. We caught them completely by surprise. As my armed horsemen rode in, the whole town panicked. In no time at all we herded the inmates together in the open yard and demanded the person of the Shehu. He came out still imagining he was the lord of his palace and the shock on his face when he saw me makes me laugh today when I think of it.

"I have come to you as you requested. But I have come to make you my prisoner," I said. "Isn't there one of your followers who will raise even a finger in defence of his master? We have captured your ragged soldiers and they are now

"I have come as you requested. But I have come to make you my prisoner." glad to be still alive."

The Shehu looked round his men and his eyes, not his mouth seemed to say: 'Won't you fight for me in spite of all I have done for you?

Are you going to let him lead me away into captivity?' But no one moved except away from him and from me and my soldiers who now wore on their faces the proud expression of victors. The followers of Shehu Minchika whose hearts were beating with fear, not knowing what I would do to them, saw clearly the end of their dependence on Shehu's charity but also the end of his ruthless and wicked domination. They saw a change coming but suspected that life would not be worse than it had been before.

I ordered the Shehu to be bound and tied to a tree while his palace was looted and valuables removed. The slaves who were waiting to be sold were set free and the Sheik's men were moved out of their cell. All the valuables were taken from the palace and tied up in big bundles. They were loaded on to the heads of the Shehu's servants and the backs of his many asses and we prepared to march out of the town towards Birnin Boko.

The Shehu looked on all these doings as if in a trance. He showed no emotion. But when I set the palace on fire, the old man wept. But he deserved and got no sympathy from anyone. This was a fitting finale to a life which was void of any virtue. And so the palace burnt; the past abode of a powerful overlord before whom everyone had bowed in awed reverence. It burnt; the palace which had been the seat of tyranny, and the scene of much callousness. The walls fell; the walls which had imprisoned innocent, bewildered and tearful children. The palace fell into ruins; the palace which was the centre of one of the biggest slave markets of all times. And as it burnt it was watched by the man who once roared like a lion and silenced everyone for miles around but now was so feeble that he could not sob aloud. And as I watched it I knew that the pride, the vanity and the callousness of this man burnt with it.

The news of the sacking of Shehu Minchika's palace soon spread into the town. No help came; no one came to the aid of the Shehu. Very few, if any, recalled any good that the Shehu had done to them and none of them were prepared to risk their lives in his defence. Many hoped for the end of his rule and looked forward to a future of greater peace and freedom.

When the news reached the Emir, in his own palace, far from seeing the attack as an assault on the most important subject of his kingdom and therefore as a challenge to him, regarded it as an act of God which had rid his kingdom of a most damnable pest. He welcomed the defeat and end of Shehu Minchika and the power, wealth and the following which he had built up over the years in defiance of and in competition with the power of the Emir. He could now look forward to a time when he could expect the loyalty, allegiance and respect of all his subjects. He had never approved of the child- stealing and slave-dealing of Shehu Minchika, but he had been powerless to do anything about it. He had pretended to ignore it therefore and had been satisfied with occasional courtesies from the Shehu when he had felt disposed to make them.

The Emir had known of the Shehu's despatch of his 'hundred' to Birnin Boko and had not doubted the success of the expedition. No one had ever escaped unhurt from the Shehu's wrath. He had been alarmed at these warlike moves of the Shehu. He feared that the Shehu's victory in Birnin Boko and the loot he would collect would further strengthen him in Garin Bassam. He had therefore set up spies to relay to him the progress of the Shehu's army.

When the unexpected happened and the Shehu's men were defeated and captured, the news reached the Emir before it reached the Shehu himself. It was an occasion of joy for the Emir for it was the first humiliation for his uncontrollable subject. The Emir's joy was complete when the news of the sacking of the palace and the capture of Shehu Minchika and his followers reached him. This he celebrated openly even while the fire was still raging in the palace. With the palace burnt down and looted, the great slave dealer himself now enslaved and his followers scattered, this threat to the Emir's position was ended. But he wanted to know more about the man who had defeated his enemy. Would the victor prove a new threat to his power?

I was about to lead my proud 'army' back home when the emissaries of the Emir came to me bearing his staff. They brought me the

greetings of the Emir and the white kola nuts
which signified an invitation to his palace. I had
already heard that there was no love lost
between the Shehu and the Emir. I knew I had
nothing to fear from this invitation. So I went,
willingly, to his palace accompanied by six of
my horsemen. The remaining horsemen took
charge of the captives and the treasure.

Nearly all the people of Garin Bassam
were gathered in front of the Emir's palace to
see and honour this valiant village man whom
the Emir had decided to honour. It was the
proudest moment in my life and in the lives of
the six who went with me. As we rode towards
the Emir where he sat in front of his palace we
were flanked by wildly cheering citizens. It was
to them like the coming of a saviour and it was
the strongest evidence yet of the hatred of the
people for the defeated Shehu.

We alighted in front of the Emir and did the necessary homage by squatting and touching the earth with our foreheads before him. Perhaps the Emir had expected to see a much older man than I, coarse in features and crude in manners; perhaps he had expected a man whose head was swollen with his recent victory and whose face was masked in the disgusting pattern of pride; and perhaps he had expected to see a man who by his manner of speech would make him, the Emir, feel small in the presence of his people. But what he saw was the exact opposite.

Before him he saw a tall, straight young man, who it was difficult to associate with the recent violence at the Shehu's place.

I could almost feel the people's hearts warming towards me as their cheers became louder. If I had been the son of the Emir they could not have given me a greater ovation. The

Emir had meant to honour me for my bravery and the services done to him and the town by ridding them of the Shehu, but now that he had seen me and the respect I accorded him, he had greater reasons for receiving me.

The Emir quickly made up his mind and conferred on me the title of: 'Shehu'. The turbaning was performed there and then.

This received general approval and Shehu Shettima was accepted and acclaimed by all. With this title was conferred all the rights and privileges which the former Shehu enjoyed. The area of land which the Shehu formerly occupied, and over part of which he built his palace, now smouldering into ashes, was allotted to me, Shehu Shettima. I was offered the citizenship of Garin Bassam and high rank among the nobles of the town. The children of Shehu Minchika who had joined him in business were banished. This was a turn of events which I had not foreseen. I thanked the Emir and the people and promised to come back in a more peaceful atmosphere before long to claim what was given me.

Amidst the cheers and goodwill of the populace I and my six men left the Emir's palace to rejoin my men and the captives. Ex-Shehu Minchika was still tied to the tree and heard from my own lips of my succession to his title and his rights. To him it must have been like reading his own obituary and watching the interment of his own corpse. There was no fight in him any longer and there was nothing to fight for. Unknown to me, he had taken a fatal drug which he had concealed in his robes, and now that drug took its effect.

He called out as loud as he could: "Listen to me for the last time, all you who still have ears to hear. See the folly of those who feel that Shehu Minchika, the terror of Garin

Bassam, can be led away lamely so that unworthy scum can have fun at his expense. A great man dies in a great way. The lion will never turn into a lamb. It shall be remembered that Shehu Minchika left this life like no other man. I am leaving now because I wish it, for I will not be led from this palace." So saying, he sank to the ground.

Those near him rushed to support him but, with a last grim smile of what he must have regarded a triumph; he made his exit from this life which he had done his utmost to deface. He probably felt that he had cheated his enemies of the joy of seeing his discomfiture, a joy which they looked forward to with a rare relish and wicked excitement. Now he was dying without pain and without any plea for mercy. Shehu Minchika in his time had often refused to heed the tearful pleas of many and he was not going to face the anguish of such a refusal himself.

And so life fled from the strong man of Garin Bassam. With him went the empty glory with which he had surrounded himself. It was the end of an era which no one wished to see again.

I and my men leading the captives, many of whom bore on their heads the treasures collected from the palace of the late Shehu Minchika, started out in the direction of Birnin Boko. We soon joined the four who still stood guard over the wounded and captured 'soldiers' of the Shehu. We had now gathered a huge crowd of surly and frightened people whose main crime was that they served and obeyed the conquered Shehu. They were frightened because they did not know what would happen to them and they thought that anyone who could overcome, and tame the terrible Minchika was sure himself to be more terrible still and that his little finger would be thicker than the thigh of the mighty Minchika.

But they were wrong. They were too blind to see that all that had happened was the natural triumph of right over wrong. They did not understand that I had done this thing in the cause of justice, not for my own greed. I had risked so much to fight and beat down injustice and slavery, and I was not now going to enslave anyone. I wanted everyone to be restored to his home where he could toil honestly for himself and even as a poor man retain the self-respect without which there is not much sense in living.

The treasures taken from Minchika's palace, which the captives carried, were now loaded onto the horses which had been ridden by my soldiers. Then I turned to the captives: "Go back and toil and labour like honest men and have pride in your own selves. Depend upon yourselves and the God whom you believe in and even in your poverty retain your pride and your freedom. You have today witnessed the end of tyranny and the reward of pride and wickedness. Keep this as a lesson and hand it on to your children. Remember that power and money corrupt excessively and excessive corruption destroys absolutely."

The people knelt and raised their hands up in praise and thanks to me, and returned home carrying with them the wounded and the weary. Their return to Garin Bassam evoked still greater acclamation for the magnanimity of Shehu Shettima of Birnin Boko and Garin Bassam.

It was already dark when I and my twenty- five followers and the laden horses and asses arrived at Birnin Boko. Our reception was one of the wildest that would ever be known in that area. We were all back with hardly a wound of war and there was I, Shettima, whose claim to renown now surpassed his grandfather's. There was no doubt in everybody's mind that the bones of Gattam Boko and of his father stirred in their graves or that they danced invisible among the jubilant villagers for the honour which I had brought on my village and my family. The women sang in praise of me and my followers, while the men drank and talked loudly.

My mother was the proudest mother ever. She slaughtered a ram to the memory of her late husband and in appreciation of the good work he had done since his death. Fatima gave me the fondest hug that any woman could give and accepted my return and achievement as if it was so ordained.

The news of the defeat of Shehu Minchika by the horse-riding heroes of Birnin Boko spread fast to neighbouring and distant villages and towns and it became a matter of pride to be born in Birnin Boko. The news of the modesty of Shettima went round too and so also the absence of desire for further conquest. No village or town feared me, for my motive for the battle against Minchika was known and approved. Everyone was grateful that children could now live in peace without fear of being kidnapped and sold to slavery.

8. The Coming of Al Atiku

But while all these things were happening, a storm was gathering in the palace of Sheik Maitama, the Lion of the Desert of Yelua. The guards had arrived with the news of the detention of two of the men sent by the Sheik to buy slaves from Shehu Minchika and of the attack on themselves. They had with them their three captives bound hand and foot. The Sheik was not only insulted by this unwarranted attack on his men but indignant at the Shehu's lack of regard for the long standing business connection between the two. The capture of the Sheik's men had decided him on the course of action to pursue. The men had to be rescued and the Shehu punished. That it might mean the end of a fruitful source of much needed labour did not enter into this reckoning.

That could take care of itself. For the time being it was not enough reason for not seeking redress for the wrong done to him.

The Sheik was too old to organise and lead an army himself but Al Atiku was of age and here was an opportunity for him to prove his manhood and also prove to the world that he deserved to succeed the Lion of the Desert when the time came. Al Atiku was more than ready for this assignment for he loved adventure and also loved to put any wrong right.

He hastily collected a fairly large fighting force from the ever-ready and willing followers of his father. They, unlike the followers of Minchika, wholeheartedly identified their interest with their master's. They were disciplined and they had a cause to fight for. Al Atiku and his men left with the blessings of all in the palace and the neighbourhood.

Led by the two slave-buying servants, they reached Garin Bassam in a record time. They made for the palace of Shehu Minchika but were stunned by the sight they saw. It was deserted and burnt. There was no one in sight. Nothing moved except the charred leaves on the stunted trees that stood here and there among the ruins.

The invaders wondered what disaster had overtaken this ignoble seat of tyranny and where the Shehu himself was. They rode among the ruins gazing at the utter destruction and wondering what hand had wrought it, robbing them of the hope of glory, the relish of victory and the joy of righting the wrong done by their master. Al Atiku was in no doubt that whatever had happened to Shehu Minchika had the hand of Allah in it and was therefore just.

They now rode towards the town and soon learnt of the fate of Shehu Minchika and his kingdom. Al Atiku smiled proudly when he heard that I had brought about the end of our common enemy. He turned around and with the help of the two servants who had come home with us, he sped towards Birnin Boko having sent back all but six of his fighting men.

His coming to Birnin Boko caused no small stir. Even before I saw Al Atiku, I knew somehow that it was him, and I was not surprised when he alighted in front of my house as I came out. It was a happy reunion between Al Atiku and me and between Al Atiku and Fatima. But the show was stolen by the two servants who had come home with Fatima and me and had stayed in the village with us. Nearly the whole village came out to greet them. Al Atiku watched with interest as the men were hugged and given warm handshakes. Right then I had a feeling that Al Atiku, friendly as he himself was, had never seen such a show of love and affection. He was to see more.

Fatima welcomed Al Atiku and I could see that she was eager to hear news of Sherifat and her old friends at the palace. It worried me to think that in the village she might have been missing the grand life of the Sheik's palace. Even though she had only been a slave girl there, she had been surrounded by wealth and entertainment, whereas now, though she was free, her life was that of a simple villager. But she quickly reassured me, telling me that this life with me was all she ever wanted. I knew too that soon I would be able to give her a new life in which she would have all the things due to the wife of a noble.

The village of Birnin Boko had not much to offer by way of excitement and activity to Al Atiku but everywhere he went he was met with smiles. The people accepted him not only because he was my friend but also because he was pleasant and kind. During his stay with us Al Atiku was very much impressed by the way we lived in the village. He saw how we moved freely together, doing things together, giving help and receiving help, yet each running his own home as he pleased. Each was free to choose and pursue any vocation he pleased and did not have to depend on anyone else. There were more smiling faces to be seen in the village than in the whole of his father's kingdom.

What was more; my people were free and were people with the same background and tradition. They gave me honour and respect not because they belonged to me, but because they loved me and singled me out on account of my merit for this love and loyalty.

Al Atiku marvelled at the speed with which I had accomplished so much. The building, the turning of young peasants into fine horsemen and the uniting of the people into one force had been achieved in a few short months. And now I have put an end to the tyranny of Shehu Minchika and won a great title for myself.

"Al Atiku spent only three days in Birnin Boko and at my invitation we proceeded on the fourth day to Garin Bassam to pay respect to the Emir who had already learnt of the coming of the son of a great sheik of the desert.

It was a delightful meeting which everyone remembered for a long time after. The Emir entertained us lavishly and we showed him much respect. Happily, his son Ahmed, who had been away from the kingdom, was now back. He was about our age and a friendship developed easily between us. Ahmed insisted that I should build on the ruin of Minchika's palace:

"What was the site of a palace of tears," he said, "should now become a palace of peace." He promised to contribute to its building for he felt that in future years, when he followed his father as Emir, my nearness and my friendship and the security which it would give would make life more pleasant and lighten his burdens. I was not given much chance to refuse for the atmosphere was too cordial for any dissension.

This posed a very big problem for me, for it meant that I would have to leave Birnin Boko to live in Garin Bassam. What would my people think and how would they take it? Leaving my home village with its comparative backwardness for the town might estrange me from them. Furthermore I had not had time to consult Fatima who in her simple purity of mind might set it down as a low ambition. I probably for the first time would have to make Fatima follow and not lead me.

A few days later Al Atiku went homeward with his six guards while I returned to Birnin Boko. Our parting was not a painful one for we knew that our visits would in the future be more frequent and our friendship still closer. Even though we did not yet know what would precipitate our meeting, we knew that it wouldn't be long before we found each in the other's loving embrace.

The news of the defeat of Shehu Minchika had reached Tulin Goma and the palace of the Sheik in Yelua days before the return of Al Atiku.

The Sheik, his nobles, the servants and the slaves had been left to create each in his own mind an image of a slave turned hero. No one seemed surprised, for although they had known me as a slave, they said I had seemed cut out for great and heroic deeds. They believed that Allah had preserved me for some great things.

When Al Atiku and his men returned with the news of my elevation to the rank of Shehu, many, like true Muslims, believed that it was all ordained from the beginning by Allah.

They longed to see me again, this time in my glory, surrounded by greatness and evidence of wealth. They wondered too about Fatima but had no doubt that she would rise to the challenge of her new life. This was the time for the Sheik to be thankful that I had been saved from a death which in fury he had ordained. Whatever reservations he might have had before, about the friendship between his noble son and the slave Shettima were now removed. What his own son laid claim to by reason of his birth, I had acquired by my unique character and singular good fortune. I was now a noble in my own right and my initial humiliation and lowliness was sunk and forgotten in a past not distant but overshadowed. If ever I returned to his palace in Yelua, I would now be accorded the rights and privileges of a nobleman.

9. Freedom for All

But the Sheik did not live long enough to meet me again, for in a few months, after a short illness, he died. He was a good man in his own way for he did not treat his slaves too badly, and, in fact, after the disaster with Matamba, of which I have spoken elsewhere, he had improved the conditions of the slaves on his plantations. And now his slaves mourned his death though they were sure that his heir, Al Atiku, was a good man who was likely to make life easier still for them.

Al Atiku suddenly became alive to the burden of responsibility which devolved on him with the death of his father. The details to be settled were many but he had a broad idea of the course he would pursue. He had no doubt that he could count on the loyalty of those who had served and ministered to his father. So his new position did not frighten him, for he had had plenty of opportunity to see how things were done. If he had been prepared to tread the same path which his father trod before him, he would have no difficulty; but he had fresh and new ideas which he meant to introduce, and he naturally wondered if they would work and if they would go down well with his people.

At first he occupied himself with arranging a fitting funeral for his father. According to the rites of their religion the old Sheik was buried within a few hours of his death but further ceremonies continued long after. Soon after the ceremonies the various activities in the Sheik's establishment were resumed with the usual devotion and application. The passing of power from father to son was hardly noticeable. No one had any misgivings about the continuity of the harmony which had existed and all accepted the new Sheik as they had accepted the old.

But the new Sheik, the young Al Atiku, was greatly agitated. This had been his plight since he returned from his reunion with me and since he saw the end of Shehu Minchika. The vanity of all the effort to amass wealth and the exploitation of other people towards this end had struck him forcibly and gnawed incessantly at him. He had seen true greatness and real happiness in me. I was not a rich man for I shared all I had with my people, but I was surrounded by people who loved me and whom I made happy in every way. I was serving them all the time, giving them advice, help and hope. They would do anything for me, not because they feared me and not because they depended upon me for their living, but because I treated them as human beings.

When he had visited the Emir of Garin Bassam, Al Atiku had seen another side of life. The Emir was different from me in that he was a rich man and well placed. He was in a position of authority and could wield his power as he liked, but he was moderate in his dealings and his subjects responded with love and reverence. Though he kept no slaves, he had all he wanted. The people who surrounded him might be poor but they lived a full life. They married and had children and lived happy family lives. No one was destined like the Sheik's slaves to wade through a life empty and without fulfillment. They were content to work for their rich overlord, but they got paid in money or in kind and so were able to fulfill their natural obligations to themselves and their families and still keep their pride.

Al Atiku would rather have himself surrounded by people like these than by those who slavishly humbled themselves before him, because they had resigned themselves to this kind of life and did not feel capable of satisfying the natural longings of a parent. Because he felt like this he resolved to put the situation right as early as possible. His father had left him a lot of money and assets and enterprises which would yield even more. Even if the introduction of the reform which he contemplated diminished what he already had, he would still be able to live in comfort and style and yet leave a great deal to his own heirs.

Al Atiku kept his own counsel but he worked out details of the reforms in his mind and waited for an opportune moment for the declaration. And he did not have to wait long. The news of the death of the Sheik had reached Birnin Boko as well as Garin Bassam. Both Ahmed, the son of the Emir, and I had been very deeply touched by this loss to our friend,

Al Atiku. We both decided that our presence in the palace at Yelua would cheer him. I wanted to pay my last respects to the Sheik and I wanted to see the initiation of my friend, Al Atiku, to the rank of a Sheik.

My coming as a titled chief and an acclaimed warrior caused a great stir among the people of Yelua. I did not come alone, I had my entourage and so too had my friend Ahmed. The palace was the scene of great festivities and soon the whole town of Yelua was infected with this goodwill towards us.

Sherifat had been delighted to hear of my coming. None of my doings and achievements had escaped her hearing. She was as proud of me as if I had been her own brother.

Like a dutiful and loving daughter, she had felt the death of her father deeply. She did not doubt that Al Atiku would provide adequately for her but it is not easy to fill the place of a loving father. Her father meant more to her than just the fountain of all the good things which she needed. His existence gave her a confidence and pride the value of which could not be expressed in terms of money and material things.

When I arrived, she threw her modesty to the winds and ran to Al Atiku's wing of the palace where she knew I would be. Cunning fate was at work and when she rushed in Al Atiku and I were in an inner room discussing the wisdom or the foolishness of the reforms which he was contemplating. She entered the large hall where her brother received his visitors and she saw there not me but a stranger: A tall, dark stranger with a long, handsome face and milk-white teeth. His carriage as he moved a few steps forwards towards her had every mark of good breeding. The stranger was Ahmed.

And Ahmed's first sight of Sherifat struck him deeply. He had met Fatima and had thought much of her. But here in front of him Ahmed saw another moon that for him shone even brighter.

For these two at that moment nothing else existed. Everything else was forgotten. The stage seemed perfectly set, as if by design, for this scene, which both were to remember throughout life.

Ahmed stepped forward towards her: "I am Ahmed, son of the Emir of Garin Bassam and you must be Sherifat, sister to Al Atiku."

"Ahmed!" she said in surprise. "But I have never heard of you. Are you a friend of Shettima? Have you come with him from Birnin Boko?"

"You are right," answered Ahmed. "I am as much a friend of Shehu Shettima as I am of the new Sheik Al Atiku."

"These new titles confound me and I guess I must get used to them. But please tell me where I may find Shettima," Sherifat said. She knew from her upbringing that it was immodest for her to be alone with a man, however much she might want to know more about him.

"He is in there with your brother. But before you go to him, may I ask you a question?" asked Ahmed.

"I should be pleased to answer your questions," answered Sherifat.

"Then I may ask it?" said Ahmed.

"But I have given you permission," answered Sherifat, surprised at the sort of question that needed so much preamble.

"It is a simple question and I hope you will not think I am rude," said Ahmed, as if he was playing for time. Sherifat began to wonder what it was all about and whether she had not thought too highly of this man who had more beauty than courage. Ahmed came out with it:

"Has anyone ever told you that you are very beautiful?" That was the question and how was Sherifat to answer it? Ahmed himself expected no answer but he simply watched her for the effect. Her shy surprise could not mask the rare pleasure that parted her lips in a smile.

He thought now he might have gone too far, and quickly changed the subject. "But you wanted to see Shettima. Wait here while I fetch the Shehu and the Sheik." But when I came out, instead of rushing into my arms and saying those affectionate things which a sister says to a homecoming brother, she smiled and stretched out her hand. I had expected a more enthusiastic welcome and a more passionate demonstration of goodwill. Her coming to see me soon after my arrival was more in keeping with this expected mood. What had dampened her enthusiasm?

I found the answer when I tried to introduce Ahmed to Sherifat.

"Sherifat, here you meet Ahmed, the son and - heir of the Emir of Garin Bassam," said I. Sherifat surprised me with her answer. "I know," she said. "We have met."

I led Sherifat away to a corner. There we sat and spoke of many things. Sherifat asked after Fatima's health and was delighted to hear that she was carrying my baby. She wished it would be a boy to follow in my footsteps. But during the long discussion I knew that something was already happening to Sherifat's heart. I had not thought of the possibility of Sherifat and Ahmed falling in love with each other but now that it was happening it seemed only natural and right.

The following day Ahmed was leading Sherifat around and soon everybody who had any sense knew that something was in the offing. Al Atiku, who now stood in the position of her father, could wish nothing better for his sister. It seemed to him as if Allah was already aiding him to put the house in order by ensuring his sister's happiness so soon after her father's death. While Allah was still at hand to help him, Al Atiku decided to put himself in His hands and take the bold step which he knew would make him and others happy. He had told me of his ideas and I had approved his plan and lauded him for his courage and goodness.

Al Atiku therefore ordered everyone in his father's establishment, be her slave, servant or freeman, to appear before him in the palace on the fourth day after our arrival. It was a large crowd that gathered in the open, outside the palace, that day. The palace yard was too small to take all of them. Al Atiku did not sit under the great colourful canopy of his father and he had no court around him. Only I, known to many, and Ahmed, who was a stranger, flanked him on either side as he rose on a platform which had been improvised for the occasion.

From this rostrum he addressed the people. He was calm and his voice was strong: "My dear people, I have called you here today in the first place to honour the memory of a great man, my father, and to take part in the celebration of the funeral ceremony. Perhaps there should be no end to according respect to the memory of the great man. But we need not mourn him any longer. We have done enough of that and why should we mourn for he was fortunate in life and he was old enough to die? There is also no occasion for you to feel sorry for yourselves for I have vowed to carry on the good work of my noble father. Perhaps I want to do a bit better.

You all remember that a short while ago, I had occasion to lead a small army from here down south towards Garin Bassam against an enemy of mankind, Shehu Minchika. You remember too that 1 and my soldiers were saved from the trouble of a fight by our old friend whom you can see on my right. We did not have to fire a gun or shoot an arrow because the job was already done by the time we arrived.

Many of my soldiers came back but I went on with a few to visit the same dear friend and to see other places.

In Garin Bassam, I saw the ruins of the places of the hated Shehu Minchika but I saw more there. I saw the Emir of that city and I made friends with his noble son whom you see on my left. I saw happy people who loved and respected their leader. They were free people. They laboured and toiled for their living but they had pride in themselves for they fulfilled their obligations to their families. I went further to Birnin Boko and I saw the same thing. I saw people with hope in life, people who have pleasure in living and exerting themselves to make life worth living. They too were free men.

I have not been able to forget all that I saw and learnt, and I do not wish to forget. Until I undertook this journey I have accepted our own way of life here. I was satisfied that since we treated our slaves and servants well we were doing enough to make them happy. But now I know better. Everyone has the right to live a full life and retain his pride; everyone has the right to marry and bring up a family in his own home, and to work for the good of his family.

I have therefore resolved to set free every slave and I declare all of you free from this moment. If you choose to return to your homes, you are free to do so at this very moment. But if you wish to stay in this establishment I am happy that you should. You will be free to give or not to give your labour, but if you do, you will be paid for it. You are free to marry like all men and if you require a piece of land to build a home apply to me and you can have land on easy terms. If you choose to live in the quarters which you already live in you will be free to do so until you get married. As time goes on you will learn more of the way these things will be organised."

The crowd did not cheer in response. They just stood there as if dazed. The news was so strange to them that very few could grasp the implications of what he was saying. All they had was a vague idea that changes were going to take place. They heard what he said about being free, but what could freedom mean to people who had lived the best part of their lives in slavery and had come to accept this as their lot. Perhaps it was even more than acceptance; they had come to like it and would, like all simple men, dread the initial hardship that change might involve. The freeing of slaves in this manner was unheard of and completely unexpected.

Al Atiku understood the confusion in their minds. He knew they needed time to take in what he had said. So, for the moment, he sent them back to their work and to the life they knew.

When after some days the meaning dawned fully on those simple people and they were able to understand the change which was to come into their lives, they marvelled at the magnanimity of the young Sheik. The people in the town heard and honoured him for placing human happiness above accumulation of wealth.

Many had feared that the freeing of slaves, by depleting the labour force on the plantations and other establishments, would spell the ruin of the enterprises and dry the fountain of wealth which had given the late Sheik much power and fame. But they were wrong. Many of the slaves remained and offered their labour for wages and worked as hard as they had ever done before.

Ahmed and I returned to Garin Bassam. But we came back before long armed with the goodwill of the Emir of Garin Bassam to celebrate the marriage of Sherifat and Ahmed. This was the final seal to a triangular friendship between a Sheik, an Emir and a Shehu. It was a friendship that was to bring peace and human dignity in the wide area that spread from Birnin Boko to Garin Bassam to Yelua, and beyond.

www.ingramcontent.com/pod-product-compliance
Lightning Source LLC
Chambersburg PA
CBHW071419300726
48976CB00004B/1170